Congressional
Research
Service

The U.N. Convention on the Elimination of All Forms of Discrimination Against Women (CEDAW): Issues in the U.S. Ratification Debate

Luisa Blanchfield
Specialist in International Relations

May 7, 2013

Congressional Research Service

7-5700

www.crs.gov

R40750

CRS Report for Congress
Prepared for Members and Committees of Congress

Summary

The Senate may consider providing its advice and consent to U.S. ratification of the United Nations (U.N.) Convention on the Elimination of All Forms of Discrimination Against Women (CEDAW, or the Convention) during the 113th Congress. CEDAW is the only international human rights treaty that specifically addresses the rights of women. It calls on States Parties to take measures to eliminate discrimination against women in all areas of life, including political participation, employment, education, healthcare, and family structure. CEDAW has been ratified or acceded to by 187 States Parties. The United States is the only country to have signed but not ratified the Convention. Other governments that have not ratified the treaty include Iran, Palau, Somalia, Sudan, and Tonga.

U.S. Actions

President Jimmy Carter signed the Convention and submitted it to the Senate in 1980. The Senate Foreign Relations Committee held hearings on CEDAW in 1988, 1990, 1994, and 2002. It reported CEDAW favorably, subject to certain conditions, in 1994 and 2002. To date, however, the Convention has not been considered by the full Senate.

The election of President Barack Obama focused renewed attention on the possibility of U.S. ratification of CEDAW. The Administration called the Convention an "important priority," and in May 2009 identified it as a treaty on which it "supports Senate action at this time." At a November 2010 hearing on CEDAW held by the Senate Judiciary Committee's Subcommittee on Human Rights and the Law, Administration officials expressed further support for U.S. ratification. Then-Ambassador-at-Large for Global Women's Issues Melanne Verveer stated that ratification is critical to U.S. efforts to promote and defend women's rights worldwide. Secretary of State John Kerry has also expressed support for U.S. ratification of CEDAW.

The Senate Foreign Relations Committee or the full Senate could consider providing its advice and consent to ratification of the Convention at any time because the treaty has already been submitted to the Senate. In practice, however, presidential support, sometimes accompanied by executive branch suggestions for conditions to ratification, has preceded Senate action.

Policy Issues

U.S. ratification of CEDAW is a contentious policy issue that has generated considerable debate in Congress and among the public.

- CEDAW supporters hold that the Convention is a valuable and effective mechanism for fighting women's discrimination worldwide. They argue that U.S. ratification would give the United States additional legitimacy when it advocates women's rights internationally, and that it might empower women who fight discrimination in specific countries.

- CEDAW opponents maintain that the treaty is not an effective mechanism for addressing discrimination against women internationally, emphasizing that countries widely believed to have poor women's rights records have ratified the Convention. Critics also contend that U.S. ratification could undermine U.S. sovereignty and impact the private conduct of U.S. citizens.

This report will be updated as events warrant.

Contents

Appendixes

Contacts

Introduction

U.S. policymakers and members of the public have contentiously debated U.S. ratification of the United Nations (U.N.) Convention on the Elimination of All Forms of Discrimination Against Women (CEDAW, or the Convention) since it was drafted in 1979. CEDAW is the only international human rights treaty that specifically focuses on the rights of women.[1] As of December 16, 2011, 187 countries have ratified or acceded to the Convention. The United States is the only nation to have signed but not ratified CEDAW. President Jimmy Carter signed the Convention and submitted it to the Senate in 1980. The Senate Foreign Relations Committee (SFRC) held hearings on CEDAW in 1988, 1990, 1994, and 2002, and reported it favorably in 1994 and 2002.[2] To date, the treaty has not been considered for advice and consent to ratification by the full Senate. Other countries that are not parties to CEDAW include Iran, Palau, Somalia, Sudan, and Tonga.[3]

The Senate may consider providing advice and consent to U.S. ratification of CEDAW during the 113th Congress. The Barack Obama Administration has expressed support for the Convention, calling it "an important priority." In a May 2009 letter to the SFRC, the Obama Administration identified CEDAW as a human rights treaty on which it "supports Senate action at this time." Most recently, Secretary of State John Kerry stated that he supported U.S. ratification of the Convention.

U.S. policymakers generally agree with CEDAW's overall objective of eliminating discrimination against women around the world. Many, however, question whether the Convention is an appropriate or effective mechanism for achieving this goal. Opponents are concerned that U.S. ratification would undermine national sovereignty and require the federal government or, worse, the United Nations to interfere in the private conduct of citizens. They argue that the Convention is ineffective, and emphasize that countries with reportedly poor women's rights records— including China and Saudi Arabia—have ratified CEDAW. Supporters, however, contend that the Convention is a valuable mechanism for fighting women's discrimination worldwide. They argue that U.S. ratification will give CEDAW additional legitimacy and empower women who aim to eliminate discrimination in their own countries.

This report addresses CEDAW's background, objectives, and structure and provides an overview of U.S. policy toward the Convention. It examines issues that have been raised in the U.S. ratification debate, including the treaty's impact on U.S. sovereignty, the effectiveness of the Convention, and its possible use as an instrument of U.S. foreign policy. It also describes controversial provisions and CEDAW Committee recommendations addressing the role of women in society and women's equal access to education and healthcare.

---

[1] Women's rights and the equality of the sexes are addressed in general terms in the Universal Declaration of Human Rights, the International Covenant on Civil and Political Rights, and the International Covenant on Economic, Social, and Cultural Rights, among others.

[2] See **Appendix B** for a timeline of SFRC consideration of CEDAW. In November 2010, the Senate Judiciary Committee Subcommittee on Human Rights and the Law held a hearing on U.S. ratification of CEDAW.

[3] See **Appendix A** for a list of countries that are parties to the Convention.

Background and Structure

U.N. member states adopted several treaties addressing aspects of women's rights prior to adoption of CEDAW in 1979, including the Convention on the Political Rights of Women (1952) and the Convention on the Consent to Marriage (1957).[4] In 1967, after two years of negotiations, the U.N. General Assembly adopted the Declaration on the Elimination of Discrimination Against Women, a non-binding document that laid the groundwork for CEDAW. Subsequently, the U.N. Commission on the Status of Women drafted CEDAW, which the General Assembly adopted on December 18, 1979.[5] The Convention entered into force on September 3, 1981, after receiving the required 20 ratifications.

Objectives

CEDAW calls on States Parties to take all appropriate measures to eliminate discrimination against women in all areas of life. This includes equality in legal status, political participation, employment, education, healthcare, and the family structure. Article 2 of the Convention specifies that States Parties should undertake to "embody the principle of equality of men and women in their national constitutions or other appropriate legislation ... to ensure, through law and other appropriate means, the practical realization of this principle." The Convention defines discrimination against women as

> any distinction, exclusion or restriction made on the basis of sex which has the effect or purpose of impairing or nullifying the recognition, enjoyment or exercise by women irrespective of their marital status, on a basis of equality of men and women, of human rights and fundamental freedoms in the political, economic, social, cultural, civil, or any other field.[6]

It specifically calls for equal pay with men, more attention to the equality of rural women, the freedom to choose a marriage partner, and the suppression of trafficking in women and girls.

The Committee on the Elimination of Discrimination Against Women

The Committee on the Elimination of Discrimination Against Women (the Committee) was established in 1982, under Article 17 of CEDAW, as a mechanism to monitor the progress of the Convention's implementation. It is composed of 23 independent experts who are elected at a meeting of States Parties to the Convention by secret ballot, with consideration given to the principle of equitable geographic distribution. Each State Party may nominate one expert, and if elected, the expert serves a four-year term.[7] The majority of the Committee members are women

---

[4] More information on international treaty bodies relating to women's rights is available at http://www.un.org/womenwatch/directory/instruments_treaties_1003 htm.

[5] The Commission on the Status of Women was established in 1946 as a functional commission of the U.N. Economic and Social Council. It is responsible for preparing recommendations and reports for the Council on women's rights in the political, economic, and social realms.

[6] Article 1, CEDAW. The text of the treaty is available at http://www.un.org/womenwatch/daw/cedaw/text/econvention htm.

[7] Some human rights treaties provide for a separate body to monitor implementation of the treaty by States Parties.

who, according to the Convention, should have "high moral standing and competence" and "represent different forms of civilization as well as principal legal systems." The Committee is led by a Chairperson, three Vice Chairpersons, and a rapporteur, which are elected by Committee members. The Chairperson directs the discussion and decision-making process of the Committee and represents the Convention at international conferences and events. The Committee reports annually on its activities to the U.N. General Assembly through the U.N. Economic and Social Council and meets twice a year at the U.N. Office in Geneva. As one of seven U.N. human rights treaty bodies, the Committee is financed from the U.N. regular budget. It was previously supported by the U.N. Division for the Advancement of Women, but since January 2008 it has been serviced by the U.N. Office of the High Commissioner for Human Rights.

The Committee is responsible for reviewing the reports on national CEDAW implementation submitted by States Parties. Countries are required to submit an initial report within the first year of ratification or accession, followed by a report every four years. The reports identify areas of progress as well as concerns or difficulties with implementation. The Committee engages in an open dialogue and exchange of ideas with the reporting country and compiles recommendations and conclusions based on its findings, which include general recommendations on cross-cutting issues of concern. The general recommendations are non-binding, and there is no mechanism for their enforcement. The Committee has made nearly 30 general recommendations since 1986 covering a wide range of issues affecting women, such as improvement in education and public information programs, elimination of female circumcision, equality in marriage and family relations, and preventing violence against women.[8]

Optional Protocol

On October 6, 1999, the U.N. General Assembly adopted an Optional Protocol to strengthen the Convention.[9] The Protocol entered into force in December 2000, and has been ratified by 104 countries. It is a stand-alone treaty that can be signed or ratified by countries that are not party to the main treaty. It includes a "communications procedure" that permits groups or individuals to file complaints with the CEDAW Committee. It also incorporates an "inquiry procedure" that allows the Committee to explore potential abuses of women's rights in States Parties to CEDAW.

U.S. Actions

Successive U.S. Administrations and Members of Congress have supported the Convention's overall objective of eliminating discrimination against women. They have disagreed, however, as to whether the Convention is an effective or appropriate means of achieving this goal.

---

[8] A full list of CEDAW Committee general recommendations can be found at http://www2.ohchr.org/english/bodies/cedaw/comments.htm.

[9] Optional Protocols sometimes accompany treaties, and are stand-alone agreements under international law.

Obama Administration Position

The Obama Administration has expressed support for the Convention. On January 15, 2009, Susan Rice, U.S. Permanent Representative to the United Nations, stated at her Senate confirmation hearing that CEDAW "will be an important priority" for the Administration.[10] In May of the same year, the Obama Administration identified CEDAW as a human rights treaty on which it "supports Senate action at this time," prompting some to speculate that the Administration may transmit the treaty to the Senate Foreign Relations Committee (SFRC) for its advice and consent.[11] In March 2010, Secretary of State Hillary Clinton announced that the Administration "will continue to work for the ratification of CEDAW."[12]

At a November 2010 Subcommittee on Human Rights and the Law hearing, then- Ambassador-at-Large for Global Women's Issues Melanne Verveer supported U.S. ratification of CEDAW, noting that it is critical to U.S. efforts to "promote and defend the rights of women" worldwide.[13] At the same hearing, Samuel Bagenstos of the Department of Justice Civil Rights Division expressed support for CEDAW ratification to "express more forcefully our [the United States'] commitment to the rights of women in the United States and to further opportunities for girls and women around the world."[14] Most recently, Secretary of State John Kerry expressed his support for U.S. ratification of CEDAW at his January 2013 nomination hearing before SFRC.[15]

> ### Steps in the U.S. Process of Making Multilateral Treaties
>
> The making of multilateral treaties for the United States involves a series of steps that generally include (1) negotiation and conclusion; (2) signing by the President; (3) transmittal to the Senate by the President, which may include any proposed reservations, declarations, and understandings; (4) referral to the Senate Committee on Foreign Relations; (5) committee consideration and report to the Senate recommending approval and a proposed resolution of ratification, which may include reservations, declarations, or understandings; (6) Senate approval of advice and consent to ratification by a two-thirds majority; (7) ratification by the President; (8) deposit of instrument of ratification; and (9) proclamation.
>
> While the House of Representatives does not participate in the treaty-making process, both chambers must act if a treaty requires implementing legislation.[1]

---

[10] Congressional Transcripts, Congressional Hearings, "Senate Foreign Relations Committee Holds Hearing on the Nomination of Susan Rice to be the U.S. Representative to the United Nations," *Congressional Quarterly*, January 15, 2009.

[11] Treaty Priority List for the 111th Congress. (Letter from Richard R. Verna, Assistant Secretary, Legislative Affairs, U.S. State Department, to Senator John F. Kerry, Chairman, Senate Committee on Foreign Relations, U.S. Senate, May 11, 2009.)

[12] U.S. Department of State, Remarks at the U.N. Commission on the Status of Women by Secretary of State Hillary Clinton, March 12, 2010. Administration officials have expressed concern regarding some aspects of the CEDAW Committee's country reports. In a November 2011 statement before U.N. member states, an Administration official stated, "There is much in those [CEDAW Committee] reports with which the United States agrees. However, there are other aspects with which we do not." (Statement by Laurie Shestack Phipps, Adviser for Economic and Social Affairs, of Position on draft resolution A/C.3/66/L.21 – CEDAW under Agenda Item 28(a) Advancement of Women, U.S. Mission to the United Nations, November 3, 2011.)

[13] Testimony of Melanne Verveer before the Senate Judiciary Committee Subcommittee on Human Rights and the Law, at the hearing, *Women's Rights are Human Rights: U.S. Ratification of CEDAW*, November 18, 2010.

[14] Testimony of Samuel R. Bagenstos of the Department of Justice Civil Division before the Senate Judiciary Committee Subcommittee on Human Rights and the Law, at the hearing, *Women's Rights are Human Rights: U.S. Ratification of CEDAW*, November 18, 2010.

[15] Congressional Quarterly Transcript, *Confirmation Hearing on the Nomination of Massachusetts Democratic Senator John Kerry to be Secretary of State*, January 24, 2013.

Previous Administration Positions

President Carter signed the Convention on July 17, 1980, and submitted it to the Senate for advice and consent on November 12 of the same year. The Reagan and first Bush Administrations did not support ratification, and the Convention remained pending in the SFRC.

Clinton Administration

The Clinton Administration supported CEDAW ratification and in 1994 sent a treaty package to the Senate for advice and consent to ratification. The package included nine proposed reservations, understandings, and declarations (RUDs) to the Convention.[16] (RUDs often accompany U.S. ratification of a treaty. See text box.) The SFRC reported the Convention favorably, but it never came to vote in the full Senate because of opposition from several Senators. The reservations recommended by the Clinton Administration addressed the following issues:

- "private conduct," which made clear that the United States "does not accept any obligation under the Convention to regulate private conduct except as mandated by the Constitution and U.S. law";

- "combat assignments," which stated that the United States "does not accept an obligation under the Convention to put women in all combat positions";[17]

- "comparable worth," which made clear that the United States would not accept the doctrine of comparable worth based on the Convention's broad description;[18] and

- "paid maternity leave," which stated that the United States could not guarantee paid maternity leave as the Convention stipulates because it is not a requirement under federal or state law.[19]

> **Reservations, Understandings, and Declarations that may Accompany U.S. Ratification of Multilateral Treaties**
>
> The Senate Committee on Foreign Relations may recommend that the Senate approve a treaty conditionally, granting its advice and consent subject to certain stipulations that the President must accept before proceeding to ratification. These stipulations are generally referred to as "Reservations, Understandings, and Declarations" (RUDs). The President may also propose RUDs at the time he transmits the treaty to the Senate or during the Senate's consideration of the treaty.
>
> *Reservations* are specific qualifications or stipulations that modify U.S. obligations without necessarily changing the treaty language.
>
> *Understandings* are interpretive statements that clarify or elaborate, rather than change, the provisions of an treaty. They are generally deemed to be consistent with the obligations imposed by the treaty.
>
> *Declarations* are statements of purpose, policy, or position related to matters raised by the treaty in question but not altering or limiting any of its provisions.

---

[16] For detailed descriptions of the RUDs, see U.S. Congress, Senate Committee on Foreign Relations, *Convention on the Elimination of All Forms of Discrimination Against Women*, Report Together with Minority Views to Accompany Ex. R, 96-2, 103rd Cong., 2nd sess., October 3 (legislative day, September 12), 1994, Senate Exec. Rept. 103-38.

[17] This reservation refers to CEDAW Article 2 that obligates States Parties to pursue "by all appropriate means ... a policy of eliminating discrimination against women."

[18] This refers to CEDAW Article 11(1)(d) that says that States Parties shall take all appropriate measures to eliminate discrimination against women in the field of employment in order to ensure "The right to equal remuneration, including benefits, and to equal treatment in respect of work of equal value, as well as equality of treatment in the evaluation of the quality of work."

[19] This reservations refers to CEDAW Article 11(2)(b) that states, "In order to prevent discrimination against women (continued...)

The three understandings submitted by the Clinton Administration stated that (1) the United States will fulfill its obligations under the Convention in a "manner consistent with its federal role," recognizing that issues such as education are the responsibility of state and local governments; (2) the United States will not accept Convention obligations that restrict freedom of speech or expression; and (3) the United States and other States Parties may decide the nature of the health and family planning services referred to in the Convention, and may determine whether they are "necessary" and "appropriate."[20] The Clinton Administration's proposed declarations included a "non-self-executing" provision, which stated that no new laws would be created as a result of CEDAW, and a "dispute settlement" provision, which stated that the United States was not bound by Convention Article 29(1) that refers unresolved disputes to the International Court of Justice.

George W. Bush Administration

The Bush Administration stated that it supported the Convention's goal of eradicating discrimination against women on a global scale but had several concerns with the Convention.[21] These concerns were outlined in 2002, when the SFRC held hearings on potential CEDAW ratification. Then-Secretary of State Colin Powell wrote a letter to the SFRC stating that the Convention was under the State and Justice Departments' review because of concerns regarding "the vagueness of the text of CEDAW and the record of the official U.N. body [the CEDAW Committee] that reviews and comments on the implementation."[22] In particular, the Administration cited "controversial interpretations" of the CEDAW Committee's recommendations to States Parties.[23] Powell's letter specifically noted a Committee report on Belarus that "questioned the celebration of Mother's Day," and a report on China that "called for legalized prostitution." These positions, Powell argued, were "contrary to American law and sensibilities."[24]

The Bush Administration further maintained that the vagueness of the CEDAW text opened the door for broad interpretation by international and domestic entities and that the 1994 RUDs proposed by the Clinton Administration did not address these interpretation issues. It also emphasized the importance of ensuring the Convention would not conflict with U.S. constitutional and statutory laws in areas typically controlled by the states.[25] In light of these concerns, the Administration urged the SFRC not to vote on the Convention until a full legal

---

(...continued)

on the grounds of marriage or maternity and to ensure their effective right to work, States Parties shall take appropriate measures ... To introduce maternity leave with pay or with comparable social benefits without loss of former employment, seniority or social allowances."

[20] For more information, see the "Family Planning" section.

[21] U.S. Mission to the United Nations press release, "Statement by Ambassador Sichan Siv, U.S. Representative to the U.N. Economic and Social Council," October 30, 2003.

[22] Letter from Colin Powell, Secretary of State, to Senator Joseph Biden, Chairman, Senate Committee on Foreign Relations, July 8, 2002.

[23] Letter from Daniel J. Bryan, Assistant Attorney General, U.S. Department of Justice, to Senator Joseph Biden, Chairman, Senate Committee on Foreign Relations, July 26, 2002.

[24] Ibid. See U.N. document, A/55/38(SUPP), p. 37, paragraph 361 (2000) for the Committee's recommendation related to Mother's Day; and U.N. document, A/54/38/REV.1(SUPP), paragraphs 288-289, January 1, 1999 for the Committee's recommendation related to prostitution.

[25] Ibid.

---

review was complete. The review began in mid-April 2002. On February 7, 2007, the Administration transmitted a letter to the Senate stating that it did not support the Senate taking action on the Convention at that time.[26]

Senate Actions

CEDAW has been pending in the SFRC for over 25 years. The committee held hearings in 1988 and 1990 but did not vote to recommend the Convention for advice and consent of the full Senate.[27] With support from the Clinton Administration, the SFRC held another round of ratification hearings in June 1994. The committee reported the Convention favorably with a vote of 13 to 5 in September 1994, but the 103rd Congress adjourned before it could be brought to vote in the full Senate.[28] The Republican Party was elected as the majority in the 104th Congress, and the incoming chairman of the Foreign Relations Committee, Senator Jesse Helms, did not allow further consideration of CEDAW because of his concerns regarding its possible impact on U.S. sovereignty and U.S. laws, including those related to abortion and family planning.[29]

In June 2002, the debate over U.S. ratification of CEDAW gained momentum as the SFRC again held hearings on ratification of the Convention. On July 30, 2002, the committee reported the Convention favorably by a vote of 12 to 7, subject to four reservations, five understandings, and two declarations.[30] These included the nine RUDs recommended by the Clinton Administration in 1994, plus two additional understandings. The first additional understanding included a proposal from Senator Jesse Helms, who was then the ranking minority Member, which stated that "nothing in this Convention shall be construed to reflect or create any right to abortion and in no case should abortion be promoted as a method of family planning." The second additional understanding addressed the impact of the CEDAW Committee on U.S. law, stating, "the CEDAW Committee has no authority to compel parties to follow its recommendations." The 107th Congress adjourned before the Senate could vote on the Convention. (See **Appendix B** for a timeline of SFRC consideration of CEDAW.)[31]

---

[26] Letter from Jeffrey T. Bergner, Assistant Secretary for Legislative Affairs, U.S. Department of State, to Senator Joseph Biden, Chairman, Senate Committee on Foreign Relations, February 7, 2007.

[27] The 1988 hearing, *Issues Relating to the United Nations Convention on the Elimination of All Forms of Discrimination Against Women*, was held before the Subcommittee on Terrorism, Narcotics and International Operations of the Senate Committee on Foreign Relations.

[28] For more information on the 1994 hearings, see U.S. Congress, Senate Committee on Foreign Relations, *Convention on the Elimination of All Forms of Discrimination Against Women*, Report Together with Minority Views to Accompany Ex. R, 96-2, 103rd Cong., 2nd sess., October 3 (legislative day, September 12), 1994, Senate Exec. Rept. 103-38.

[29] For more information on Senator Helms' position, see U.S. Congress, Senate Committee on Foreign Relations, *Convention on the Elimination of All Forms of Discrimination Against Women*, Report Together with Minority Views to Accompany Ex. R, 96-2, 103rd Cong., 2nd sess., October 3 (legislative day, September 12), 1994, Senate Exec. Rept. 103-38, pp. 53-54. Moreover, in 2000, Senator Helms stated, "if I have anything to do with it [CEDAW ratification] – and I think I do – it will never see the light of day on my watch." Senate, *Congressional Record*, vol. 146 (May 11, 2000), p. S3926.

[30] U.S. Congress. Senate. Committee on Foreign Relations, "Convention on the Elimination of All Forms of Discrimination Against Women," Report, September 6, 2002. Washington, DC, Government Printing Office (Senate Exec. Rept. 107-9, 107th Cong., 2nd sess.), pp. 7-11.

[31] During the 111th Congress, the Senate Judiciary Committee Subcommittee on Human Rights and the Law held a hearing on CEDAW entitled, *Women's Rights Are Human Rights: U.S. Ratification of the Convention on the Elimination of All Forms of Discrimination Against Women (CEDAW)*.

On November 18, 2010, the Senate Judiciary Committee's Subcommittee on Human Rights and the Law held a public hearing, "Women's Rights Are Human Rights: U.S. Ratification of the Convention on the Elimination of All Forms of Discrimination Against Women (CEDAW)," representing the first Senate hearing on CEDAW in eight years. Witnesses included Melanne Verveer, then-Ambassador-at-Large for Global Women's Issues at the Department of State; Samuel R. Bagenstos, Principal Deputy Assistant Attorney General at the Department of Justice; Wazhma Frogh of the Afghan Women's Network; Marcia D. Greenberger of the National Women's Law Center; actress and activist Geena Davis; and Steven Grove of The Heritage Foundation.

Though it has no direct role in providing advice and consent to ratification of treaties, the House of Representatives has demonstrated a continued interest in CEDAW. In January 2013, Representative Lynn Woolsey introduced H.Res. 19 expressing the sense of the House of Representatives that the Senate should ratify the Convention. As of May 7, 2013, the resolution has 57 cosponsors. Similar House resolutions were introduced in the 106th through 112th Congresses.

Issues and Policy Options for the Senate

Some policy decisions and issues may continue to play a role in the debate if the Senate considers providing its advice and consent to ratification during the 113th Congress.

Possible Impact on U.S. Sovereignty

For many policymakers, the question of U.S. ratification of CEDAW touches on the broader issue of national sovereignty. The minority views in the 2002 SFRC report on the Convention, for instance, state that CEDAW represents "a disturbing international trend" of favoring international law over U.S. constitutional law and self-government, thereby undermining U.S. sovereignty.[32] Opponents are particularly concerned that if the United States ratifies the Convention, the CEDAW Committee would have authority over the actions of the U.S. government and private citizens regarding discrimination against women. Many critics, for example, have taken issue with the Committee's recommendations regarding abortion, Mother's Day, and prostitution.[33]

CEDAW advocates maintain that U.S. ratification would not affect national sovereignty. During Senate debate in 2002, for instance, proponents argued that the Convention would impose a "minimal burden" on the United States given that the Constitution and other existing federal and state laws already meet the obligations of the Convention.[34] Supporters also emphasize that the

---

[32] U.S. Congress, Senate Committee on Foreign Relations, *Convention on the Elimination of All Forms of Discrimination Against Women*, Report Together With Minority and Additional Views to Accompany Treaty Doc. 96-53, 107th Cong., 2nd sess., September 6, 2002, Exec. Rept. 107-9, p. 16.

[33] See, for instance, Patrick F. Fagan, *How U.N. Conventions on Women's and Children's Rights Undermine Family, Religion, and Sovereignty*, Heritage Foundation, Backgrounder 1407, Washington, DC, February 5, 2001, at http://www.heritage.org/research/internationalorganizations/bg1407.cfm.; and Wendy Wright, *CEDAW Committee Rulings*, Concerned Women for America, August 27, 2002.

[34] U.S. Congress, Senate Committee on Foreign Relations, *Treaty Doc. 96-53; Convention on the Elimination of All Forms of Discrimination Against Women, Adopted by the U.N. General Assembly on December on December 18, 1979, and Signed on Behalf of the United States of America on July 17, 1980*, Hearing Before the Committee on Foreign Relations, 107th Cong., 2nd sess., June 13, 2002, S. Hrg. 107-530, p. 3.

United States would likely file several reservations, understandings, and declarations (RUDs) to the Convention, including a non-self-executing declaration that would require Congress to enact implementing legislation to bring CEDAW's provisions into use—thereby addressing any potential conflicts with existing U.S. laws. Advocates further contend that the actions of the CEDAW Committee would not affect domestic laws or the private lives of U.S. citizens. They maintain that the Committee relies primarily on individual countries to fulfill their obligations under the Convention and that it has no established rules for enforcing its recommendations or addressing treaty non-compliance.[35] In order to alleviate ongoing concerns regarding the Committee's role, during the 2002 Senate ratification debate then-SFRC Chairman Senator Joseph Biden proposed an understanding stating the CEDAW Committee does not have the authority to compel States Parties to follow its recommendations.

Effectiveness of the Convention

A major point of contention among supporters and opponents of U.S. ratification is whether CEDAW is an effective mechanism for addressing women's rights internationally. Opponents generally recognize that global discrimination against women is a problem that should be eliminated, but they do not view the Convention as an effective way to achieve this goal. They emphasize that many countries widely believed to have poor women's rights records ratified the Convention. In support of this view, critics point to Saudi Arabia, a State Party to CEDAW, which does not allow women to vote, even though such a policy contradicts Article 7 on political participation.[36] Some also contend that the Convention hurts rather than helps women struggling to achieve human rights internationally—arguing that CEDAW serves as a "facade for continuing atrocities" in countries that have ratified it.[37]

Supporters of U.S. ratification maintain that CEDAW is an effective mechanism for improving women's rights globally. They contend that the Convention is a formal mechanism through which to draw attention to women's issues on both a national and international level, particularly in developing countries.[38] To support this position, they cite studies and research conducted on CEDAW's implementation. The U.N. Development Fund for Women (UNIFEM) (now UN Women), for example, found that some countries, including Brazil and Colombia, incorporated language into their national constitutions to reflect CEDAW provisions or objectives.[39] In June

---

[35] See Leila Rassekh Milani, Sarah C. Albert, and Karina Purushotma, *CEDAW: The Treaty for the Rights of Women - Rights that Benefit the Entire Community*, Working Group on the Ratification of CEDAW, Washington, DC, p. 50; and American Bar Association, *Convention on the Elimination of All Forms of Discrimination Against Women: Fear vs. Fact*, Washington, DC, April 19, 2009.

[36] See Helen Jones and Kas Wachala, "Watching Over the Rights of Women," *Social Policy and Society*, vol. 5, no. 1 (2006), pp. 129-130; and Human Rights Watch, *Saudi Arabia: Women's Rights Promises Broken*, July 8, 2009.

[37] U.S. Congress, Senate Committee on Foreign Relations, *Treaty Doc. 96-53; Convention on the Elimination of All Forms of Discrimination Against Women, Adopted by the U.N. General Assembly on December on December 18, 1979, and Signed on Behalf of the United States of America on July 17, 1980*, Hearing Before the Committee on Foreign Relations, 107th Cong., 2nd sess., June 13, 2002, S. Hrg. 107-530, p. 15.

[38] See, for example, a January 3, 2013, letter from over 100 non-governmental and women's rights organizations to Members of the U.S. Senate urging ratification of CEDAW during the 113th Congress and noting that "CEDAW is already making a difference worldwide," at http://cedaw2013.org/index.php/component/content/article/68; and "Op-Ed: Senate Needs to Ratify the Treaty for the Rights of Women," by Senators Joseph Biden and Barbara Boxer, *San Francisco Chronicle*, June 13, 2002.

[39] UNIFEM further reported that CEDAW was cited in court decisions related to women's rights in Australia, Colombia, Costa Rica, and India. See *Bringing Equality Home: Implementing the Convention on the Elimination of All Forms of Discrimination Against Women*, edited by Ilana Landsber-Lewis, UNIFEM, 1998.

2000, York University and the International Women's Rights Project (IWRP) conducted the First CEDAW Impact Study, which highlighted evidence of CEDAW's effectiveness at the national level and identified circumstances that contributed to successful implementation of the Convention. The study found that in Turkey CEDAW was cited in numerous court cases regarding discrimination against women; while in Nepal, the Ministry of Women and Social Welfare formed a taskforce to review all laws that were inconsistent with the Convention.[40] In addition, a 2010 study by the International Center for Research on Women found that:

- in **Saudi Arabia**, CEDAW is being used to draft a new law that allows women lawyers to try family cases in court (under current law they cannot do so);

- in the **Philippines** in 2009, the government introduced the Magna Carta of Women (Republic Act No. 9710), a comprehensive women's rights law that relies heavily on CEDAW provisions and definitions;

- in **Costa Rica** in 2003, the Constitutional Chamber of the Supreme Court ruled that the Legislative Assembly President had not named a proportionate number of women to the Assembly's permanent committees, which was inconsistent with the Costa Rican constitution and Article 7 of CEDAW; and

- in **Zambia** in 1997, the High Court ruled in Longwe v. Intercontinental Hotels that the Intercontinental Hotel discriminated against women under the Zambian constitution and Articles 1, 2, and 3 of CEDAW because it refused to allow women to enter the premises unaccompanied by a male companion.[41]

Despite such progress, supporters have acknowledged that much work needs to be done to achieve full implementation of CEDAW. In particular, the IWRP impact study identified several barriers to the Convention's implementation, including (1) the alienation of national governments from civil society, (2) lack of support from governments, (3) difficulty in implementing gender-integrated policies, and (4) lack of public awareness. Similarly, UNIFEM acknowledged that CEDAW's effectiveness is "largely dependent on the political will of governments."[42]

Both supporters and opponents of U.S. ratification have expressed concern with some of the RUDs filed by States Parties that appear to undermine the intent and effectiveness of the treaty.[43] For instance, several countries—including Egypt, Iraq, Malaysia, and Syria—submitted reservations stating that certain provisions would not apply if they are deemed incompatible with Islamic Shari'a law or values. Similarly, Niger filed a reservation to a provision calling on States Parties to modify social and cultural patterns related to the conduct of men and women, while

[40] *The First CEDAW Impact Study: Final Report*, York University Centre for Feminist Research and the International Women's Rights Project, June 2000, available at http://www.iwrp.org/CEDAW_Impact_Study.htm.

[41] Drawn from Ann Warner, *Recognizing Rights, Promoting Progress, The Global Impact of the Convention on the Elimination of All Forms of Discrimination Against Women (CEDAW)*, International Center for Research on Women, Washington, DC, 2010.

[42] *Bringing Equality Home: Implementing the Convention on the Elimination of All Forms of Discrimination Against Women,* edited by Ilana Landsber-Lewis, UNIFEM, 1998, p. 9. In addition, the American Bar Association (ABA) Rule of Law Initiative, in collaboration with USAID, has developed assessments tools measuring CEDAW implementation in specific countries, including Armenia, Georgia, Russia and Serbia.

[43] See, for instance, "U.S. Ratification of Human Rights Conventions: The Ghost of Senator Bricker," by Louis Henkin, *The American Journal of International Law*, vol. 89:431, (April 1995) pp. 341-350; and "Making CEDAW Universal: A Critique of CEDAW's Reservation Regime under Article 28 and the Effectiveness of the Reporting Process," by Jennifer Riddle, *George Washington University International Law Review*, vol. 34, (2002) pp. 605-638.

North Korea filed a reservation to a provision that calls on States Parties to modify or abolish existing laws that constitute discrimination against women.[44] When filing their own reservations, other States Parties—including Canada, France, and the United Kingdom—formally objected to the inclusion of these reservations, stating that they conflict with Article 28(2) of CEDAW, which states that a reservation incompatible with the object and purpose of the Convention shall not be permitted.[45]

Many CEDAW proponents acknowledge the concerns regarding RUDs; however, they maintain that the benefits of the Convention's almost universal ratification outweighs the drawbacks of conditions imposed by some States Parties.[46] Supporters also emphasize that a number of governments have decided to withdraw or modify RUDs because their national laws, policies, or priorities have changed. Examples of countries that have withdrawn reservations include the Bahamas, France, Germany, and Ireland.[47]

CEDAW as an Instrument of U.S. Foreign Policy

CEDAW proponents contend that U.S. ratification will increase the credibility of the United States abroad and enhance its ability to champion women's rights in other countries.[48] They argue that U.S. non-ratification leads other governments to question the U.S. commitment to combating discrimination against women, thereby hindering its ability to advocate women's rights internationally. For example, at a 2010 hearing before the Senate Subcommittee on Human Rights and the Law, then-Ambassador Verveer stated that CEDAW non-ratification "deprives us [the United States] of a powerful tool to combat discrimination against women ... because as a non-party, it makes it more difficult for us to press other parties to live up to their commitments under the treaty."[49] At the same hearing, Wazhma Frogh, a women's rights activist from Afghanistan,

---

[44] States Parties that filed similar RUDs regarding Islamic law include Bahrain, Kuwait, Libya, Maldives, Mauritania, Monaco, Morocco, Oman, Pakistan, and the United Arab Emirates. See Article 5(a) for Niger, and Article 2(f) for North Korea.

[45] Denmark, for instance, objected to the reservations of Bahrain, Saudi Arabia, and Syria which stated that CEDAW would not apply if it was not in accordance with Islamic law. Austria, Canada, the Czech Republic, France, and the United Kingdom filed objections to similar reservations made by other Islamic countries. Finland, France, and Portugal objected to the reservations filed by North Korea, while Denmark and Norway objected to the reservations of Niger.

[46] Specifically, some argue that maximizing the number of countries that ratify human rights treaties such as CEDAW may also enhance the force and impact of national laws developed as a result of a country's ratification. See Catherine Logan Piper, "Reservations to Multilateral Treaties: The Goal of Universality," *University of Iowa Law Review,* vol. 71, (1985) p. 1.

[47] For example, the Bahamas withdrew reservations related to Article 16 (equality in marriage and family relations); France withdrew reservations related to Article 7 (equality in political and public life), Article 15 (equality under the law), and Article 16; Germany withdrew reservations related to Article 7; Ireland withdrew reservations related to Article 9 (equal right to nationality), Article 11 (equality in employment), Article 13 (equality in economic and social life), and Article 15. Other countries that have withdrawn reservations include New Zealand, South Korea, and the United Kingdom. A list of RUDs and withdrawals are available at http://treaties.un.org/Pages/ViewDetails.aspx?src= TREATY&mtdsg_no=IV-8&chapter=4&lang=en#28.

[48] A 2002 SFRC report, for example, states that the United States should support ratification because it would "give our [U.S.] diplomats a tool ... to press other governments to fulfill their obligations under the Convention." See U.S. Congress. Senate. Committee on Foreign Relations, "Convention on the Elimination of All Forms of Discrimination Against Women," Report, September 6, 2002. Washington, DC, Government Printing Office (Senate Exec. Rept. 107-9, 107th Cong., 2nd sess.), p. 5. Also see Nancy F. Kaufman, "New Tools for Mideast Peace," *The Hill,* March 18, 2013.

[49] The Ambassador also noted that "Some governments use the fact that the U.S. has not ratified the treaty as a pretext for not living up to their own obligations under it." Testimony of Melanne Verveer before the Senate Judiciary Committee Subcommittee on Human Rights and the Law, at the hearing, *Women's Rights are Human Rights: U.S.* (continued...)

---

stated that U.S. failure to ratify CEDAW "is of huge international significance," and noted that conservative elements in Afghanistan "use American's failure to ratify CEDAW to attack [Afghan] women's rights defenders."[50]

Supporters also maintain that the United States might be viewed as hypocritical because it expects countries to adhere to international standards that it does not itself follow.[51] In support of this position, some point to U.S. statutes that require foreign assistance to be based on a recipient country's compliance with "internationally recognized human rights."[52] Many also hold that U.S. ratification would give the United States additional fora in which to combat discrimination against women, particularly if a U.S. citizen were elected to the CEDAW Committee. Serving on the Committee, supporters argue, would provide the United States with an opportunity to share its expertise and experience in combating discrimination against women with other countries.[53]

Critics contend that the United States is already an international leader in promoting and protecting women's rights and that CEDAW ratification would not affect its ability to advocate such issues internationally.[54] They argue that current U.S. laws and policies regarding gender discrimination serve as an example of the United States' commitment to women's equality. In addition, many assert that CEDAW and, more broadly, other human rights treaties, are meant for countries with lesser human rights records than the United States.[55] Some critics have also voiced reluctance to bring the question of U.S. obligations under international human rights treaties to other countries, particularly those with poor human rights records. Many opponents are also concerned that the CEDAW Committee could be used as a platform for unfounded political criticisms of the United States.[56] Moreover, they contend that U.S. ratification would not affect

---

(...continued)

Ratification of CEDAW, November 18, 2010.

[50] Testimony of Wazhma Frogh of the Afghan Women's Network before the Senate Judiciary Committee Subcommittee on Human Rights and the Law, at the hearing, *Women's Rights are Human Rights: U.S. Ratification of CEDAW,* November 18, 2010.

[51] "The Charade of U.S. Ratification of International Human Rights Treaties," by Kenneth Roth, Executive Director of Human Rights Watch, *Chicago Journal of International Law,* Fall 2000. In addition, Human Rights Watch stated in a June 13, 2002, letter to the SFRC, "By ratifying CEDAW, the U.S. government will be in a stronger position to support women's rights.... Having not ratified CEDAW, U.S. intervention in support of women's rights may be construed as 'cultural imperialism' or an 'American' agenda, as opposed to a rights-based approach."

[52] For instance, §116(a) of the Foreign Assistance Act of 1961, as amended (P.L. 87-195) states, "No assistance may be provided ... to the government of any country which engages in a consistent pattern of gross violations of internationally recognized human rights." Similarly, §502B(a)(1) of that Act states, "a principal goal of the foreign policy of the United States shall be to promote the increased observance of internationally recognized human rights by all countries." Further, §502B(a)(2) states, "no security assistance may be provided to any country the government of which engages in a consistent pattern of gross violations of internationally recognized human rights."

[53] Leila Rassekh Milani et al., *CEDAW: The Treaty for the Rights of Women - Rights that Benefit the Entire Community,* Working Group on the Ratification of CEDAW, Washington, DC, p. 18.

[54] Prepared statement of Steven Groves of The Heritage Foundation before the Senate Judiciary Committee Subcommittee on Human Rights and the Law, at the hearing, *Women's Rights are Human Rights: U.S. Ratification of CEDAW,* November 18, 2010.

[55] Christopher J. Kicka and William A. Estrada, *Special Report: The U.N. Convention on the Rights of the Child, The Most Dangerous Attack on Parent's Rights in the History of the United States,* Home School Legal Defense Association, November 1, 1999, updated March 2007.

[56] See Rebecca J. Cook, "Reservations to the Convention on the Elimination of Discrimination Against Women," *Virginia Journal of International Law,* vol. 30, (1990) p. 643; and Belinda Clark, "The Vienna Convention Reservations Regime and the Convention on Discrimination Against Women," *American Journal of International Law,* vol. 85, (April 1991) pp. 281-321.

the laws and policies addressing discrimination against women in other countries. They further emphasize that improvements in the status of women in nations such as China and Sudan can be made only by the governments of these countries.[57]

Family Structure and Parental Rights

Many opponents of CEDAW are concerned that U.S. ratification would undermine U.S. privacy laws and policies—particularly those relating to family structure and the rights and responsibilities of parents.[58] Some, for example, have taken issue with provisions that they believe could be interpreted to undermine traditional family roles. Article 5(a), for instance, calls on States Parties to take all appropriate measures

> (a) To modify the social and cultural patterns of conduct of men and women, with a view to achieving the elimination of prejudices ... which are based on ... the idea of the inferiority or the superiority of either of the sexes or on stereotyped roles for men and women;

> (b) To ensure that family education includes ... recognition of the common responsibility of men and women in the upbringing and development of their children, it being understood that the interest of the children is the primordial consideration in all cases.

Such language has prompted critics to contend that CEDAW obligates governments, families, and individuals to adhere to a predetermined or artificial set of values, regardless of whether they align with national law, family traditions, or personal convictions. Specifically, some argue that the Convention dismisses "established moral and ethical principles" that are based on human nature and experience, and discriminates against the "traditional" family and a "diversity of cultures and religious beliefs."[59]

CEDAW proponents counter that the Convention does not obligate States Parties to redefine or regulate gender roles or family structures. They note that Article 5 calls on States Parties to take "all *appropriate* measures" [emphasis added], thereby leaving it to governments to determine what actions are appropriate based on their domestic laws and policies.[60] Some further argue that Article 5 addresses gender stereotypes in the context of their possible link to violence against women. To support this position, they point to the CEDAW Committee General Recommendations on Violence Against Women. Recommendation 19, for instance, relates "traditional attitudes by which women are regarded as subordinate to men or as having stereotyped roles" to "practices involving violence or coercion."[61] Consequently, some contend,

---

[57] U.S. Congress. Senate. Committee on Foreign Relations, "Convention on the Elimination of All Forms of Discrimination Against Women," Report, September 6, 2002. Washington, DC, Government Printing Office (Senate Exec. Rept. 107-9, 107th Cong., 2nd sess.), p. 54.

[58] Laurel MacLeod and Catherina Hurlburt, *Exposing CEDAW: Concerned Women for America Strongly Opposes CEDAW,* Concerned Women for America, September 5, 2000.

[59] "Women for Faith and Family Statement on the United Nations Convention on the Elimination of All Forms of Discrimination Against Women," Women for Faith and Family, May 25, 2000.

[60] Testimony of Marcia D. Greenberger of the National Women's Law Center before the Senate Judiciary Committee Subcommittee on Human Rights and the Law, at the hearing, *Women's Rights are Human Rights: U.S. Ratification of CEDAW,* November 18, 2010.

[61] CEDAW Committee General Recommendation 19 (11th session, 1992). Also see General Recommendation 12 (8th session, 1989).

Article 5(b) addressing family planning education primarily refers to public education, grant, or information programs that aim to combat violence against women.[62]

Another area of concern is CEDAW's possible impact on the role of women as mothers and caregivers. Many opponents are particularly critical of the CEDAW Committee's recommendation to Belarus in 2000 that expressed concern regarding the "continuing prevalence of sex-role stereotypes and by the reintroduction of such symbols as a Mother's Day ... which it sees as encouraging women's traditional roles."[63] Some point to this statement as evidence of CEDAW redefining the family and the role of women in society.[64] In response to such concerns, supporters argue that the Committee was not criticizing Mother's Day; rather, it was responding to Belarus's celebration of the holiday as the only response to the obstacles women face in that country. Proponents further emphasize that the Committee has reviewed the reports of many other countries that celebrate Mother's Day and made no similar comments.[65]

A number of critics also contend that U.S. ratification of CEDAW may undermine parental rights. Opponents have taken issue with Article 16(d), which says that States Parties shall take all appropriate measures to ensure that women receive "the same rights and responsibilities as parents ... in matters relating to their children; in all cases the interest of the children shall be paramount."[66] Opponents are concerned that such language could be interpreted to give the CEDAW Committee authority to determine what is in the best interest of U.S. children, thereby undermining the rights and responsibilities of parents.[67] Proponents, however, contend that CEDAW supports the role of parents in child-rearing, emphasizing that it calls for the "common responsibility of men and women in the upbringing and development of their children."[68] Furthermore, they argue that CEDAW would not affect parental rights because the U.S. Constitution limits government interference in private matters, including parenting.[69]

Recognizing the concerns of many CEDAW opponents regarding the Convention's possible impact on the private lives of U.S. citizens—particularly relating to family and parenting—in 1994 the Clinton Administration proposed a "private conduct" reservation to the Convention. It stated that the United States "does not accept any obligation under the Convention to regulate private conduct except as mandated by the Constitution and U.S. law."[70] Some CEDAW

---

[62] Leila Rassekh Milani et al., *CEDAW: The Treaty for the Rights of Women - Rights that Benefit the Entire Community*, Working Group on the Ratification of CEDAW, Washington, DC, p. 51.

[63] U.N. document, A/55/38(SUPP), p. 37, paragraph 361 (2000).

[64] See Laurel MacLeod and Catherina Hurlburt, *Exposing CEDAW, Concerned Women for America strongly opposes CEDAW*, Concerned Women for America, September 5, 2000; and U.S. Senate Republican Policy Committee, *Why a Pro-Women Senate Should Not Ratify CEDAW*, August 14, 2002.

[65] Testimony of Marcia D. Greenberger before the Senate Judiciary Committee Subcommittee on Human Rights and the Law, at the hearing, *Women's Rights are Human Rights: U.S. Ratification of CEDAW*, November 18, 2010.

[66] Leila Rassekh Milani et al., *CEDAW: The Treaty for the Rights of Women - Rights that Benefit the Entire Community*, Working Group on the Ratification of CEDAW, Washington, DC, pp. 54, 61-62.

[67] See, for instance, *Women for Faith and Family Statement on the United Nations Convention on the Elimination of All Forms of Discrimination Against Women*, Women for Faith and Family, May 25, 2000. Similar language is included in Article 5(b), which says that States Parties shall take all appropriate measures to recognize "the common responsibility of men and women in the upbringing and development of their children, it being understood that the interest of the children is the primordial consideration in all cases."

[68] Article 5(b), CEDAW.

[69] American Bar Association, *Convention on the Elimination of All Forms of Discrimination Against Women: Fear vs. Fact*, Washington, DC, April 19, 2009.

[70] U.S. Congress, Senate Committee on Foreign Relations, *Convention on the Elimination of All Forms of* (continued...)

---

supporters object to the inclusion of the proposed reservation, arguing that the United States should strive to adhere to the treaty's provisions regarding gender stereotypes. They contend that a private conduct reservation implies a "lack of political commitment" by the United States and indicates that it views CEDAW as "applicable only in other countries."[71]

Abortion

A significant issue in the CEDAW ratification debate centers on whether the Convention takes a position on abortion or is "abortion neutral." Many who support U.S. ratification hold that the treaty is abortion neutral because the word "abortion" is never mentioned in the Convention's text. This point of view was shared by the Clinton Administration, which declared the treaty abortion neutral in 1994.[72] Supporters also emphasize that many countries where abortion is regulated or illegal, including Burkina Faso, Colombia, and Ireland, ratified the Convention without associated reservations, understandings, or declarations (RUDs), and regularly report to the CEDAW Committee.[73]

Many opponents of U.S. ratification argue that while CEDAW does not include the word "abortion," parts of the Convention text could be interpreted to undermine current U.S. abortion law. Specifically, some have taken issue with Article 12(1), which states that countries "shall take all appropriate measures to eliminate discrimination against women in the field of health care in order to ensure ... access to health care services, including those related to family planning." Critics have also expressed concern regarding Article 16(1)(e), which requires that States Parties take all appropriate measures to ensure that women have the right to "decide freely and responsibly on the number and spacing of their children." Opponents suggest that such language could lead to the abolishment of state parental notification laws, require federal funding for abortions, or obligate the U.S. government to promote and provide access to abortion.[74] Two States Parties to the Convention—Malta and Monaco—explicitly stated in their reservations to CEDAW that they do not interpret Article 16(1)(e) as imposing or forcing the legalization of abortion in their respective countries.

(...continued)

Discrimination Against Women, Report Together with Minority Views to Accompany Ex. R, 96-2, 103rd Cong., 2nd sess., October 3 (legislative day, September 12), 1994, Senate Exec. Rept. 103-38. This reservation was also included in 2002 when the SFRC reported the Convention favorably in July of that year.

[71] National Organization for Women (NOW), *Legal Analysis of CEDAW RDUs: Joint Position of the Lawyers Committee for Human Rights and the NOW Legal Defense Fund*, September 26, 1994, available at http://www.now.org/issues/global/cedaw_analysis.html.

[72] Prepared Testimony of Jamison S. Borek, Deputy Legal Adviser, U.S. Department of State, on U.S. Ratification of CEDAW. U.S. Congress, Senate Committee on Foreign Relations, *Convention on the Elimination of All Forms of Discrimination Against Women (Ex. R, 96-2)*, Hearing Before the Committee on Foreign Relations, 103rd Cong., 2nd sess., October 27, 1994, S. Hrg. 103-892, p. 13.

[73] See Leila Rassekh Milani et al., *CEDAW: The Treaty for the Rights of Women - Rights that Benefit the Entire Community*, Working Group on the Ratification of CEDAW, Washington, DC, pp. 59-60; and American Bar Association, *Convention on the Elimination of All Forms of Discrimination Against Women, Fear vs. Fact*, April 19, 2009.

[74] Letter from Douglas Johnson, Legislative Director, National Right to Life Committee (NRLC), and Jeanne E. Head, R.N., Vice President for International Affairs, NRLC, to Members of the U.S. Senate, March 25, 2009; and Grace Smith Melton, *CEDAW: How U.N. Interference Threatens the Rights of American Women*, Heritage Foundation, Backgrounder No. 2227, Washington, DC, January 9, 2009.

CEDAW supporters counter such criticisms by emphasizing that Articles 12 and 16 call on States Parties to take all "*appropriate* measures" [emphasis added], thereby leaving it up to States Parties to determine what actions are appropriate based on their domestic laws and policies. To support this view, some have cited the negotiating history of CEDAW,[75] which appears to demonstrate the intent of some countries to keep the Convention's text intentionally ambiguous so that the treaty could be ratified by countries with a wide range of domestic laws and policies.[76]

CEDAW Committee Recommendations Related to Abortion

The CEDAW Committee's recommendations to States Parties regarding abortion are a particularly controversial aspect of the U.S. ratification debate. Many opponents of CEDAW, particularly pro-life advocates, are strongly critical of the Committee because, in their view, it calls on States Parties to support and encourage abortion despite the fact that it is never mentioned in the CEDAW text.[77] As evidence of this, critics point to the Committee's General Recommendation 24, which elaborates on CEDAW Article 12(1) addressing women's equal access to health care, including family planning services. The Committee recommends that "when possible, legislation criminalizing abortion could be amended to remove punitive provisions imposed on women who undergo abortion."[78] Opponents also criticize Committee recommendations to individual countries that appear to encourage the decriminalization or legalization of abortion and oppose conscientious objector policies. In 1998, for example, the Committee recommended to Mexico that "all states ... should review their legislation so that, where necessary, women are granted access to rapid and easy abortion."[79] More recently, in 2007, the Committee urged Poland "to ensure that women seeking legal abortion have access to it, and that their access is not limited by the use of the conscientious objection clause."[80] In addition, opponents have suggested that the Committee's interpretation of CEDAW could be used as a basis for challenging abortion laws in the United States and other countries. In particular, some critics have expressed concern with a May 2006 decision by the Constitutional Court of Colombia, which cited CEDAW when it determined that abortion should not be considered a crime in all circumstances (such as rape or incest and when the life of the mother is in danger).[81]

---

[75] According to international law, a treaty may be interpreted by taking into account the preparatory work and negotiations related to the treaty text. Specifically, Article 32 of the 1969 Vienna Convention on the Law of Treaties states, "Recourse may be had to supplementary means of interpretation, including the preparatory work of the treaty and the circumstances of its conclusion, in order to confirm the meaning resulting from the application of Article 31, or to determine the meaning when the interpretation according to Article 31: (a) leaves the meaning ambiguous or obscure; or (b) leads to a result which is manifestly absurd or unreasonable." The United States signed the Vienna Convention on April 24, 1970, but the Senate has not given its advice and consent to ratification. According to the State Department, the United States "considers many of the provisions of the Vienna Convention on the Law of Treaties to constitute customary international law on the law of treaties."

[76] See, for instance, U.N. document, A/C.3/33/L.47/Add.2*, December 4, 1978, paragraph 223, "Introducing his amendment, the representative of Bahrain stated that its intention was to allow a wide range of understanding, since it was important that [CEDAW] articles on civil and family rights be consistent with national laws."

[77] Wendy Wright, *CEDAW Committee Rulings - Examples of U.N. CEDAW Committee Rulings Reveal How Dangerous the Treaty Would be to Americans,* Concerned Women for America, August 27, 2002.

[78] CEDAW Committee General Recommendation 24, 20th session, 1999, at http://www.un.org/womenwatch/daw/cedaw/recommendations/recomm.htm#recom24.

[79] U.N. document, A/53/38/Rev.1, May 14, 1998.

[80] U.N. document, CEDAW/C/POL/CO/6, February 2, 2007.

[81] Ioana Ardelean, *An Ominous Sampling of International Efforts to Force Abortion on Reluctant Nations*, Culture of Life Foundation, at http://culture-of-life.org//content/view/497/1/. Excerpts from the Colombian Court's decision (C-(continued...)

As mentioned previously, many CEDAW supporters emphasize that the purpose of the Committee is to consider the progress of States Parties' implementation of the Convention. They point out that CEDAW has no established mechanism for non-compliance and that it relies primarily on States Parties to fulfill their treaty obligations.[82] Further, proponents contend that many of the Committee recommendations to States Parties demonstrate its overall opposition to abortion as a method of family planning. In 2006, for example, the Committee expressed concern that in the Former Yugoslav Republic of Macedonia "abortion continues to be used as a method of birth control."[83] Similarly, in 2007 the Committee noted with concern that in Greece "due to inadequate access to family planning and contraceptive methods, abortion is often used by women and adolescent girls as a method of birth control."[84] Moreover, supporters maintain that the overall goal of the Committee is to encourage States Parties to reduce abortion rates through education and family planning. Consequently, some argue, the Committee makes recommendations regarding abortion only in very specific circumstances, such as when (1) a nation demonstrates a high rate of abortion, indicating that voluntary family planning education and resources are needed to reduce the abortion rate; (2) a country appears to rely on abortion as a method of family planning; or (3) a country reports that unsafe and illegal abortions contributed to high mortality rates.[85]

The U.S. "Helms Understanding" on Abortion (2002)

In June 2002, under the chairmanship of former Senator Joseph Biden, the SFRC held hearings on CEDAW ratification. On July 30, 2002, the committee reported the Convention favorably by a vote of 12 to 7, subject to several RUDs. One of the understandings was a proposal from Ranking Member Senator Jesse Helms that stated "nothing in this Convention shall be construed to reflect or create any right to abortion and in no case should abortion be promoted as a method of family planning."[86] This "Helms understanding" was included as a compromise to alleviate the concerns of pro-life advocates who were concerned that CEDAW ratification could affect U.S. abortion laws.

Though some pro-choice women's groups favoring U.S. ratification questioned whether the understanding was necessary or appropriate, they recognized that its inclusion could increase the chances of U.S. ratification—which they believed would improve the lives of women both domestically and abroad. Conversely, other women's groups that supported U.S. ratification opposed the inclusion of the Helms understanding because, in their view, it would encourage

---

(...continued)

355/06) are available at http://www.womenslinkworldwide.org/pdf_pubs/pub_c3552006.pdf.

[82] Leila Rassekh Milani et al., *CEDAW: The Treaty for the Rights of Women - Rights that Benefit the Entire Community*, Working Group on the Ratification of CEDAW, Washington, DC, pp. 59-60.

[83] U.N. document, CEDAW/C/MKD/CO/3, February 3, 2006, paragraph 31.

[84] U.N. document, CEDAW/C/GRC/CO/6, February 2, 2007, paragraph 25. Also see paragraph 36 of U.N. document, CEDAW/C/CTI/CO/7, February 10, 2009, addressing Haiti, which states that the Committee is concerned at the "frequent use of abortion as a family planning measure."

[85] Leila Rassekh Milani et al., *CEDAW: The Treaty for the Rights of Women - Rights that Benefit the Entire Community*, Working Group on the Ratification of CEDAW, Washington, DC, pp. 59-60.

[86] U.S. Congress. Senate. Committee on Foreign Relations, "Convention on the Elimination of All Forms of Discrimination Against Women," Report, September 6, 2002. Washington, DC, Government Printing Office (Senate Exec. Rept. 107-9, 107th Cong., 2nd sess.), p. 7. The "Helms understanding" was originally proposed in 1994. (See Senate Exec. Rep. 103-38, 103rd Cong., 2nd sess., p. 52.)

---

countries that have ratified CEDAW to view it as abortion neutral. They argued that such an interpretation could add legitimacy to efforts of other governments that prohibit abortion and infringe on women's reproductive rights.[87]

Some pro-life opponents of U.S. ratification were satisfied that the Helms understanding would address their concerns regarding the Convention's impact on U.S. abortion laws. Many, however, believed that it would fail to ensure that domestic abortion laws would not be affected by U.S. ratification. In particular, they argued that abortion should be addressed as a "reservation" to the Convention instead of as an "understanding." (An understanding is an interpretive statement that is generally considered to have less authority than a reservation under international law.) Some also suggested that the inclusion of the Helms understanding would have no impact on the recommendations of the CEDAW Committee. They further argued that the understanding would most likely not prevent pro-choice organizations from advocating for fewer abortion restrictions in the United States.[88]

Family Planning

A number of CEDAW opponents are concerned with specific references to family planning in the Convention text, including the following:

- Article 10(h), addressing education, calls on States Parties to take all appropriate measures to ensure "access to specific educational information to help and ensure the health and well-being of families, including information and advice on family planning." Many fear that this could lead to mandatory sex education in both public and private U.S. schools.[89]

- Article 12(1), addressing healthcare, calls on States Parties to take all appropriate measures to "eliminate discrimination against women in the field of health care in order to ensure, on a basis of equality of men and women, access to health care services, including those related to family planning."[90] Many are concerned that such language could require the U.S. government to distribute family planning materials or contraceptives at schools or in public. Some also assert that CEDAW's references to access to family planning could be interpreted to include abortion.[91]

---

[87] See Global Justice Center, *False Choices, Sacrificing Equality to Get CEDAW (Draft Version)*, November 9, 2007; and Joanna Pozen, *The High Price of Compromise*, RH Reality Check, September 18, 2007.

[88] See Letter from Douglas Johnson, Legislative Director, National Right to Life Committee (NRLC), and Jeanne E. Head, R.N., Vice President for International Affairs, NRLC, to Members of the U.S. Senate, March 25, 2009, Women for Faith and Family, *WFF Statement on the United Nations Convention on the Elimination of All Forms of Discrimination Against Women*, May 25, 2000; and Laurel MacLeod and Catherina Hurlburt, *Exposing CEDAW, Concerned Women for America Strongly Opposes CEDAW*, Concerned Women for America, September 5, 2000.

[89] Some have also expressed concern regarding CEDAW Committee recommendations regarding sex education. On January 28, 2002, for instance, the Committee urged Russia to "include sex education in the school curriculum." See U.N. document, A/57/38. For further examples, see Wendy Wright, *CEDAW Committee Rulings*, Concerned Women for America, August 27, 2002.

[90] In addition, Article 12(2) states, "States Parties shall ensure to women appropriate services in connection with pregnancy, confinement and the post-natal period, granting free services where necessary, as well as adequate nutrition during pregnancy and lactation."

[91] See Letter from Douglas Johnson, Legislative Director, National Right to Life Committee (NRLC), and Jeanne E. Head, R.N., Vice President for International Affairs, NRLC, to Members of the U.S. Senate, March 25, 2009; and (continued...)

- Article (12)(2) calls on States Parties to "ensure to women appropriate services in connection with pregnancy, confinement and the post-natal period, granting free services where necessary, as well as adequate nutrition during pregnancy and lactation." Some interpret this to mean that the U.S. government could be required to pay for family planning services, including abortion.

- Article 14(2)(b), addressing problems faced by rural women, calls on States Parties to take all appropriate measures to "have access to adequate health care facilities, including information, counseling and services in family planning." The concerns regarding this provision are similar to those expressed regarding Article 12(1).

CEDAW supporters counter these concerns by emphasizing that the Convention calls on States Parties to take "all *appropriate* measures" [emphasis added], thereby leaving it to governments to determine what constitutes access to family planning. In support of this, they point to the negotiating history of the Convention that indicates that the text was left intentionally ambiguous to allow for states with different family planning policies to ratify the Convention.[92] To address the concerns of some Convention opponents, in 1994 the Clinton Administration proposed an understanding to CEDAW that said that the United States

> understands that Article 12 permits States Parties to determine which health care services are appropriate in connection with family planning, pregnancy, confinement, and the post-natal period, as well as when the provision of free services is necessary, and does not mandate the provision of particular services on a cost-free basis.[93]

Proponents argue that such an understanding allows for the United States to provide its own interpretation of family planning; however, others counter that its inclusion is "superfluous" because the CEDAW text already provides for such interpretations through its use of the terms "appropriate" and "necessary."[94]

Consideration of Other Treaties

The Senate may consider providing its advice and consent to other treaties during the 113th Congress—including the U.N. Convention on the Law of the Sea, the U.N. Convention on the Rights of the Child (CRC), and the U.N. Convention on the Rights of Persons with Disabilities (CRPD).[95] These treaties, like CEDAW, have generated considerable debate because of concerns

---

(...continued)

Women for Faith and Family, *CEDAW Action Alert*, August 22, 2002.

[92] According to accounts of CEDAW's negotiating history, "Some countries were opposed to the mention of 'family planning services' in paragraph 1 [of Article 12], since these did not exist everywhere and it could result in the refusal to ratify the convention." See Lars Adam Rehof, *Guide to the Trauvaux Preparatoires of the United Nations Convention on the Elimination of All Forms of Discrimination Against Women* (The Netherlands: Martinus Nijhoff Publishers, 1993), p. 145.

[93] This understanding was also included in the list of RUDs accompanying CEDAW when it was reported favorably by the SFRC on July 30, 2002. See Senate Exec. Rept. 107-9, 107th Cong., 2nd sess., p. 12.

[94] National Organization for Women (NOW), *Legal Analysis of CEDAW RDUs: Joint Position of the Lawyers Committee for Human Rights and the NOW Legal Defense Fund*, September 26, 1994.

[95] For more information on CRC and CRPD, see CRS Report R40484, *The United Nations Convention on the Rights of the Child*, by Luisa Blanchfield, and CRS Report R42749, *The United Nations Convention on the Rights of Persons with Disabilities: Issues in the U.S. Ratification Debate*, coordinated by Luisa Blanchfield.

---

that they might undermine U.S. sovereignty and affect current U.S. laws and policies. In particular, the debate over U.S. ratification of CRC, which aims to protect the rights of children, includes many issues similar to CEDAW—including the Convention's possible effect on education, parental rights, and healthcare. Unlike CEDAW, however, CRC has not been submitted to the Senate by the President. Consequently, the Senate cannot yet consider providing its advice and consent to ratification.

Options for Treaties Already Submitted to the Senate

The Senate Foreign Relations Committee (SFRC) or the full Senate could consider providing its advice and consent to ratification of the Convention at any time because the treaty has already been submitted to the Senate. In practice, however, presidential support, sometimes accompanied by executive branch suggestions for conditions on ratification, has preceded Senate action. For example, the Senate considered the Convention on the Prevention and Punishment of the Crime of Genocide, the Convention Against Torture and Other Cruel, Inhuman or Degrading Treatment or Punishment, and the International Covenant on Civil and Political Rights after being strongly urged to do so by Presidents Reagan (with respect to Genocide and Torture) and George H. W. Bush (with respect to Torture and Civil and Political Rights).

Options for the Senate include the following:

- The SFRC continuing to take no action on CEDAW. The treaty may be left as it currently stands, as pending SFRC business, with the Senate neither giving nor rejecting advice and consent to ratification.

- The Senate giving its advice and consent to ratification without recommending any reservations, understandings, and declarations (RUDs).

- The Senate giving its advice and consent subject to the RUDs proposed by previous Administrations (Presidents Carter and Clinton) and/or by the current Administration.

- The Senate giving its approval for advice and consent, with RUDs proposed by the SFRC or by Members on the Senate floor.

- The Senate rejecting the treaty if more than one-third of the Senators present vote against U.S. ratification.

- The Senate requesting, by resolution, that the Convention be withdrawn and sent back to the President without any action.

Other Issues in the Ratification Debate

A number of other issues may arise in the CEDAW ratification debate if the Senate considers providing its advice and consent to ratification during the 113th Congress. These issues involve the effect of the Convention on the private conduct of citizens, as well as its impact on current U.S. laws and policies.

Decriminalization of Prostitution

Article 6 of CEDAW says that States Parties shall take all appropriate measures, including legislation, to "suppress all forms of traffic of women and exploitation of prostitution of women." Some critics contend that the CEDAW Committee has made recommendations that contradict the intent of this provision and could obligate States Parties to decriminalize or legalize prostitution.[96] Specifically, in 1999 the Committee expressed its concern in a report on China that prostitution "which is often a result of poverty and economic deprivation, is illegal," and recommended that it be decriminalized by the Chinese government.[97] Supporters, however, assert that the Convention does not support prostitution, and emphasize that the Committee made the recommendation in an effort to reduce high levels of prostitution in China. They argue that regulating prostitution might make it easier for prostitutes who are victims of violence to come forward without fear of retaliation or shame, undergo treatment for sexually transmitted diseases, or receive access to education.[98]

Definition of Discrimination

CEDAW opponents argue that the Convention's definition of discrimination against women is too broad and that it could apply to private organizations and areas of personal conduct not covered by U.S. law.[99] A primary point of contention is the use of the phrase "any other field," which some interpret to mean that CEDAW could interfere in the private lives of individuals—including family life or religious practices. Critics have also expressed concern that such a broad definition could lead to an increase in "frivolous" lawsuits.[100] Supporters, however, hold that the CEDAW definition of violence against women would not undermine U.S. laws regarding discrimination, particularly if the Senate files a non-self-executing declaration stating that no new laws would be created as a result of the treaty's ratification. They also emphasize that U.S. ratification of the International Convention on the Elimination of All Forms of Racial Discrimination (CERD), which includes a definition of racism, did not lead to an increase in the number of lawsuits.[101] Still others maintain that applying the CEDAW definition to U.S. law would improve domestic

---

[96] Prepared statement of Steven Groves of The Heritage Foundation before the Senate Judiciary Committee Subcommittee on Human Rights and the Law, at the hearing, *Women's Rights are Human Rights: U.S. Ratification of CEDAW*, November 18, 2010.

[97] U.N. document, A/54/38 (Part I), May 4, 1999, p. 32, paragraphs 288-289.

[98] Leila Rassekh Milani et al., *CEDAW: The Treaty for the Rights of Women - Rights that Benefit the Entire Community*, Working Group on the Ratification of CEDAW, Washington, DC, p. 52.

[99] Article 1 of CEDAW defines discrimination against women as "any distinction, exclusion or restriction made on the basis of sex which has the effect or purpose of impairing or nullifying the recognition, enjoyment or exercise by women irrespective of their marital status, on a basis of equality of men and women, of human rights and fundamental freedoms in the political, economic, social, cultural, civil, or any other field."

[100] Women for Faith and Family, *Women for Faith and Family Statement on the United Nations Convention on the Elimination of All Forms of Discrimination Against Women*, May 25, 2000.

[101] CERD defines racial discrimination as "any distinction, exclusion, restriction or preference based on race, color, descent, or national or ethnic origin which has the purpose or effect of nullifying or impairing the recognition, enjoyment or exercise, on an equal footing, of human rights and fundamental freedoms in the political, economic, social, cultural or any other field of public life." It entered into force on January 4, 1969, has been ratified or acceded to by 173 U.N. member states. It was ratified by the United States on October 21, 1994, and entered into force on November 20 of the same year.

discrimination laws; however, they acknowledge that to do so would likely require separate action by Congress or the Administration.[102]

Equal Access to Education

Some opponents have taken issue with CEDAW provisions addressing equal access to education. Specifically, Article 10(b) calls on States Parties to take all appropriate measures to ensure that men and women receive "access to the same curricula ... examinations, teaching staff with qualifications of the same standard and school premises and equipment of the same quality." Some contend that this provision could require U.S. parents to send their children to public schools instead of single-sex schools, private schools, or home schools. Some have also expressed concern with Article 10(d), which calls on States Parties to ensure "the elimination of any stereotyped concept of the roles of men and women at all levels and in all forms of education ... by the revision of textbooks and school programs and the adaptation of teaching methods." Some critics hold that implementation of this provision might lead to "gender re-education" in U.S. schools that could include re-writing curricula to reflect gender neutrality.[103] CEDAW supporters argue that the intent of the text is to ensure that girls and boys have equal access to education services, facilities, and curricula, regardless of whether they attend a single or mixed-sex school. They also note that CEDAW does not specifically mention single-sex schools.[104]

Same-Sex Marriage

Some CEDAW opponents who oppose same-sex marriage hold that Article 1, which defines discrimination against women as "any distinction, exclusion or restriction made on the basis of sex," could obligate the United States to legalize same-sex marriage because not allowing a woman to marry another woman could be viewed as a form of discrimination.[105] Others, however, maintain that CEDAW's aim is to address discrimination against women rather than men. Consequently, they argue, a same-sex marriage claim in the context of CEDAW would be ineffective because the treaty applies only to women.[106]

---

[102] See Leila Rassekh Milani et al., *CEDAW: The Treaty for the Rights of Women - Rights that Benefit the Entire Community*, Working Group on the Ratification of CEDAW, Washington, DC, p. 51; and American Bar Association, *Convention on the Elimination of All Forms of Discrimination Against Women: Fear vs. Fact*, April 19, 2009.

[103] Laurel MacLeod and Catherina Hurlburt, *Exposing CEDAW, Concerned Women for America strongly opposes CEDAW*, Concerned Women for America, September 5, 2000.

[104] Amnesty International USA, *Support the Treaty for the Rights of Women (CEDAW): Fact Versus Fiction*, 2009.

[105] Grace Smith Melton, *CEDAW: How U.N. Interference Threatens the Rights of American Women*, Heritage Foundation, Backgrounder No. 2227, Washington, DC, January 9, 2009.

[106] American Bar Association, *Convention on the Elimination of All Forms of Discrimination Against Women: Fear vs. Fact*, April 19, 2009. Proponents also point out that many countries that have ratified CEDAW have banned same-sex marriage. For more information, see CRS Report RL31994, *Same-Sex Marriages: Legal Issues*, by Alison M. Smith.

Appendix A. States Parties to the Convention on the Elimination of All Forms of Discrimination Against Women

Afghanistan	Central African Republic	Georgia*
Albania*	Chad	Germany*
Algeria	Chile	Ghana*
Andorra*	China	Greece*
Angola*	Colombia*	Grenada
Antigua and Barbuda*	Cook Islands*	Guatemala*
Argentina*	Comoros	Guinea
Armenia*	Congo	Guinea-Bissau*
Australia*	Costa Rica*	Guyana
Austria*	Cote d'Ivoire*	Haiti
Azerbaijan*	Croatia*	Honduras
Bahamas	Cuba	Hungary*
Bahrain	Cyprus*	Iceland*
Bangladesh*	Czech Republic*	India
Barbados	Democratic People's Republic of Korea	Indonesia
Belarus*	Democratic Republic of the Congo	Iraq
Belgium*	Denmark*	Ireland*
Belize*	Djibouti	Israel
Benin	Dominica	Italy*
Bhutan	Dominican Republic*	Jamaica
Bolivia*	Ecuador*	Japan
Bosnia & Herzegovina*	Egypt	Jordan
Botswana*	El Salvador	Kazakhstan*
Brazil*	Equatorial Guinea*	Kenya
Brunei Darussalam	Eritrea	Kiribati
Bulgaria*	Estonia	Kuwait
Burkina Faso*	Ethiopia	Kyrgyzstan*
Burundi	Fiji	Lao Peoples Democratic Rep.
Cambodia*	Finland*	Latvia
Cameroon*	France*	Lebanon
Canada*	Gabon*	Lesotho*
Cape Verde*	Gambia	Liberia

Libyan A. Jamahiriya*	Pakistan	Suriname
Liechtenstein*	Papua New Guinea	Swaziland
Lithuania*	Paraguay*	Sweden*
Luxembourg*	Peru*	Switzerland*
Madagascar	Philippines*	Syrian Arab Republic
Malawi	Poland*	Tajikistan
Malaysia	Portugal*	Thailand*
Maldives*	Qatar	The former Yugoslav Republic of Macedonia*
Mali*	Republic of Korea*	Timor-Leste*
Malta	Republic of Moldova*	Togo
Marshall Islands	Romania*	Trinidad and Tobago
Mauritania	Russian Federation*	Tunisia*
Mauritius*	Rwanda*	Turkey*
Mexico*	Saint Kitts and Nevis	Turkmenistan*
Micronesia	Saint Lucia	Tuvalu
Monaco	St. Vincent & the Grenadines	Uganda
Mongolia*	Samoa	Ukraine*
Montenegro*	San Marino*	United Arab Emirates
Morocco	Sao Tome and Principe	United Kingdom*
Mozambique*	Saudi Arabia	United Republic of Tanzania*
Myanmar	Senegal*	Uruguay*
Namibia*	Serbia*	Uzbekistan
Nauru	Seychelles*	Vanuatu*
Nepal*	Sierra Leone	Venezuela*
Netherlands*	Singapore	Viet Nam
New Zealand*	Slovakia*	Yemen
Nicaragua	Slovenia*	Zambia
Niger*	Solomon Islands*	Zimbabwe
Nigeria*	South Africa*	
Norway*	Spain*	
Oman	Sri Lanka*	
Panama*	St. Kitts and Nevis*	

Source: U.N. Office of the High Commissioner for Human Rights.

Note: * = ratified or acceded to the Optional Protocol.

Appendix B. Senate Committee on Foreign Relations Consideration of CEDAW: Timeline and Documentation

- **November 12, 1980**—Convention on the Elimination of All Forms of Discrimination Against Women, adopted by the U.N. General Assembly on December 18, 1979, and signed on behalf of the United States of America on July 17, 1980. Ex. R, 96-2. (Treaty Doc. 96-53.)

- **December 5, 1988**—Public hearing. (S. Hrg. 100-1039.)

- **August 2, 1990**—Public hearing. (S. Hrg. 101-1119.)

- **September 27, 1994**—Public hearing. (S. Hrg. 103-892.)

- **September 29, 1994**—Ordered reported, 13 in favor, 5 against.

- **October 3, 1994**—Reported, with four reservations, four understandings, and two declarations, and with minority views. (Exec. Rept. 103-38.)

(Automatically re-referred under Paragraph 2 of Rule XXX of the Standing Rules of the Senate.)

- **June 13, 2002**—Public hearing. (S. Hrg. 107-530.)

- **July 25, 2002**—Discussion during business meeting.

- **July 30, 2002**—Ordered reported, 12 in favor, 7 against.

- **September 6, 2002**—Reported with four reservations, five understandings and two declarations. (Exec. Rept. 107-9.)

(Automatically re-referred under paragraph 2 of Rule XXX of the Standing Rules of the Senate.)

Sources: Senate Committee on Foreign Relations, CRS.

Notes: Due to Senate computerization of Executive Clerk records, all treaties must conform to the same numbering system. In the case of treaties prior to the 97th Congress, the new treaty number is denoted in parentheses. All votes are by voice unless otherwise indicated.

Author Contact Information

Luisa Blanchfield
Specialist in International Relations
lblanchfield@crs.loc.gov, 7-0856